Hilbre Island in Medieval Times

some legends revisited

by

Susan Craggs

A version of this article was published in
Cheshire History in 2004

To

JDC and DEMC

First Published 2010 by Countyvise Ltd.
14 Appin Road, Birkenhead, Wirral. CH41 9HH

Copyright © 2010 Susan Craggs

The right of Susan Craggs to be identified as the author of this work has been asserted by her in accordance with the Copyright, Design and Patents Act 1988.

British Library Cataloguing in Publication Data.
A catalogue record for this book is available from the British Library.

ISBN 978 1 906823 37 5

All rights reserved. No part of this publication may be reproduced, stored in a retrieval system, or transmitted, in any other form, or by any other means, electronic, chemical, mechanical, photocopying, recording or otherwise, without the prior permission of the publisher.

Hilbre is one of 3 small islands in the mouth of the River Dee, lying between Wales and Wirral. Its present area is about 11 acres, a third of this being bare rock. The name is also used jointly for the group of islands, the smallest being Little Eye, also called The Eye. The middle-sized one is known as Middle Eye, Middle Hilbre, or (confusingly) Little Hilbre.

Hilbre, the Dee estuary, and north Wirral

Only the main island has been inhabited in historic times. The present buildings date mainly from 1841 to early 20th century.[1]

Little earlier remains, probably because structures on the sheltered eastern side of the island have been rebuilt many times, destroying or re-using parts of older buildings, such as the medieval chapel.

19th century houses, probably built on the site of the medieval chapel and cottage

The writer's researches since the 1980s were directed to discovering from the archives the probable sequence of events on the islands, and their contexts. As the search progressed, the legends (many of them dating only from Victorian antiquaries' accounts, such as those of Hume and Ecroyd Smith) became more clearly revealed as mistaken attempts to explain what was known about Hilbre's recorded or anecdotal past at that time, without the background of information which later became available. Unfortunately, the legends have already given rise to the dedication of a nearby church, and are often quoted as historical facts by modern writers. The truth is hard to establish, as records were lost, or never kept in the first place. Any account of Hilbre's past has to be told with caution, but there are some useful clues. Hilbre, despite being an isolated group of islands, was not separated from the politics and economics of the mainland, nor of medieval England as a whole. Its affairs were connected with those of the Norman barons of Cheshire, local abbeys, and the development of shipping in the Dee.

Chester Cathedral, the former Abbey of St. Werburgh

After Henry VIII dissolved Chester Abbey in 1540, its documents of land ownership, grants, leases and court cases were scattered for a while. In the 19th and 20th centuries much of the information relating to Chester Abbey was re-assembled, translated from Latin and published, allowing a more detailed study of medieval affairs in the district.[2]

Later maps and sailing instructions gave additional clues to buildings visible in Wirral and on Hilbre, such as charts by Fearon and Eyes.[3] Little archaeological evidence of medieval times survived, except 2 grave markers, ash and pottery, and reports of objects found on the islands and the nearby shore, written mainly in the mid-nineteenth century.[4]

Recent excavations found pieces of early floor tiles. Some of the antiquaries' stories can now be reassessed, in the light of later research.

Hilbre floor tile
(photograph by Colin Jones)

The first legend: The place name

The earliest written version of Hilbre's name appeared in a grant of about 1140, in which it was given as Hildeburgheye, the Saxon for Hildeburgh's Island.[5]

Spellings since then include Hildeburghee, Helbre, Helbrey and Hilbree. It was not until the Rev. Hume wrote his book on Ancient Meols in 1863 that the name was interpreted specifically as Saint Hildeburgh's island.[6] He described artefacts found on the North Wirral shore, which he took as proof of a medieval pilgrimage. Henry Ecroyd Smith continued to make this assumption nearly 10 years later in his articles about the supposed grave yard and the church on the island, which he ascribed to St. Hildeburgh.[7]

In fact, the Oxford Dictionary of Saints lists no-one in Britain called Hildeburgh. Similar names were Aldeburgh, a saint who apparently lived as an anchoress near Muncaster in Cumbria, and Hildeburgh in Germany. There may be a resemblance between the late 7th century nun, St. Ermengild or Ermenhild, the widowed mother of St. Werburgh. Although St. Werburgh became the patron saint of Chester Abbey and its predecessor, a college of canons founded in about 910, she never visited this part of Mercia as a living woman. Her coffin was reportedly carried to Chester from Hanbury in Staffordshire, some 200 years after her death in about 700, in order to protect her remains from the Danish invasion.[8] The tomb of her mother, Ermenhild, is probably still at Ely, where she died as a widowed queen and nun in the Saxon abbey.

15th century picture of St. Ermenhild and other Ely nuns, at the burial of St. Etheldreda, reproduced by kind permission of the Society of Antiquaries of London

If the island's name is simply Hildeburgh's Island, we wonder who the lady was. Some of the Norman landowners after Williams I's Conquest in 1066 were already familiar with Britain, according to the chronicles of Orderic Vitalis, as they had sometimes travelled here in the time of the Saxon King Edward.[9] This was true of King William himself, who claimed that the childless Saxon King Edward had promised to make William his heir.

Certainly Hugh Lupus, Earl of Chester, had a Saxon step mother, and her name was given (although not reliably) by Ormerod in 1819 as Ermenhild, a relative of the last Saxon Earl of Mercia.[10] Perhaps Hilbre was named in her honour. Hilbre and part of the Wirral mainland were in the barony of Robert of Rhuddlan, a cousin of Hugh Lupus.

Where an island had been dedicated to a saint, the title was often included in its name, for example St. Mary's (Island) both in Scilly and at Whitley Bay in Northumberland. Hume and Ecroyd Smith considered the chapel on Hilbre to be St. Hildeburgh's, whereas medieval documents clearly attributed it to St. Mary, also called the Blessed Virgin, and Our Lady.

The second legend: The Pilgrimage

John Leland, visiting Wirral in about 1540 as a chronicler for Henry VIII, described Hilbre as having had a former pilgrimage to Our Lady of Hilbre.[11] At the time of Henry's reformation of the English church, pilgrimages were discouraged, and would be closed down altogether a few years later, under Henry's son Edward VI. The nearby pilgrimage to St. Winefride at Holywell in Flintshire continued illegally. But this was paid for by pilgrims being caught and punished in the later 16th century, and inn keepers penalised for sheltering illicit guests. The guidebook celebrates the survival of the shrine through the times of persecution to the present day, claiming it to be the only medieval shrine in Britain with such an unbroken record of visits.

To be a pilgrim or to follow the Old Religion of Roman Catholicism was for a while treated in the same way as being a political traitor. Leland at the time of his visit in 1540 missed seeing Hilbre's festival by at least 4 years, and possibly for longer. There is no indication when the 'pilgrimage' had ceased, but it was obviously still in the local memory. Its object, the chapel of Our Lady (the Virgin Mary) was also remembered.

In medieval times, pilgrimages were not only journeys undertaken to receive a spiritual enlightenment. They were also technically defined as visits which earned benefits. The relics of a saint could cure certain ills; St. Werburgh's girdle in Chester Abbey was put on by women who wanted to conceive.[12] In addition, there was forgiveness of sins, indulgences, which brought money to the church, and were criticised as confidence tricks by some of the early Protestant reformers. Even Chaucer hinted that his Pardoner was selling false indulgences.

Whichever purpose was attached to a pilgrimage, it had to have the sanction of a Pope, or his representative in Britain. The Papal Registers and Letters include no such permission for Hilbre to host a pilgrimage.[13] It is possible that the local people, enjoying an annual visit to hear Mass at the island chapel on 15th August, the Festival of the Assumption, called it their own local 'pilgrimage'. The writer has still to check whether a medieval Archbishop of Canterbury sanctioned a pilgrimage here, as the Pope's agent.

In 1922, J. Tait published a collection of documents which had once belonged to Chester Abbey.[14] After the Reformation, and the establishment of Chester Cathedral in the old abbey buildings (and with staff largely made up of the redundant monks), the medieval land leases would have been useful for a while as proof of title. As the centuries passed, and new agreements replaced the older ones, many of the documents were lost, used as recycled writing material, or passed to the new lessees of Cathedral lands. Some land owners kept their parchments in the family chest, while many were bought by antiquaries, such as the Cotton family. Eventually some of the collections went to the Public Record Office or to college libraries, where they are now stored. Many others were lost, but as there were frequent copies and confirmations of former charters or deeds, a useful series remains in Chester's archive, especially when translated from the Latin originals.

Few of these would have been accessible to either Hume or Ecroyd Smith. Even as experienced historians, they would have found little archival evidence to explain their discoveries. In any case, the Victorians loved a good story, or a good ancestral tree, and sometimes ignored the dull reality. The important contribution of these two antiquarians is the recording in their books and articles of artefacts, some of which have since disappeared.

Among the Abbey's records is an agreement to relinquish certain rights over Hilbre, from the early

1230s.[15] Dating of documents was not a priority in these times. The year of the king's reign was often cited, or there may be national or local references which narrow down the time of the document, such as the names of witnesses. The 1230s document is possibly a clue to the origin of the "Pilgrimage". The background was complicated, as the reasons for its existence began nearly 90 years before. The Earls of Chester held the advowson or right to appoint rectors to the two churches of West Kirby parish, St. Bridget's in the village, and the dependent chapel of St. Mary on Hilbre. In about 1140, Earl Ranulph II had appointed his clerk, Nigel, to the post.[16]

St Bridget's Parish Church, West Kirby

This was a period when clergy were still sometimes married, but the Roman Catholic church discouraged this practice, and had expressly forbidden it at the second Lateran Council of 1139.[17] Firstly, the church cited many precedents for a celibate clergy. Secondly, if hereditary priesthoods became established, the church lands would pass out of direct control of the church and fall into the power of the priests' descendants. This was evidently happening in West Kirby, whether the rectors were clergy (but married), or simply the lay employers of ordained curates, and claiming the property rights of rectors for their families.

The rectors, descended from Nigel for the next 3 generations until the 1230s, claimed both the advowson (right to appoint clergy) and the glebe land, the priests' portion of the parish lands.[18] They may have been secular rectors, not in holy orders, a practice which still partly survived in some post medieval parishes. In these places the landowner's family paid an ordained clergyman to hold services, and maintained the eastern end of the church building. Peatling Magna in Leicestershire was probably one example. The parishioners were expected to pay for repairing the western part of the building, out of their tithes or church taxes.[19]

West Kirby's supposed tithe barn on Rectory Brow

Records do not reveal the exact nature of Nigel's married status, but list his family's names, including William, who was his grandson or great nephew.[20] Nigel's descendants were probably legitimate, as there was no challenge to their inheritance on these grounds. The quitclaim in the 1230s stated that William renounced all rights to the island of Hildeburghey with its chapel and appurtenances, except for the offerings at a service on the Feast of the Assumption of the Blessed Mary, and the right to perform all burials at the mother church of West Kirby.[21] This annual service for the local parishioners would be their 'pilgrimage', a walk of about two miles over the shore on a summer day, to the island's chapel.

St. Alban's, Worcester, a small Saxon chapel

Apparently William died shortly after this. Earl Ranulph III appointed his own chancellor as rector to West Kirby, and then immediately handed the advowson to Chester Abbey, effectively bowing out of the quarrel with William's descendants.[22] It was probably about this time that Chester Abbey placed Hilbre in its own parish of St. Oswald, an ancient institution of Chester city. The church was part of the fabric of the Abbey buildings, at this time in the south nave aisle, and later taking up the whole south transept.[23] When the Abbey became the new Chester Cathedral in 1541 it retained the freehold title to Hilbre, and even though the island's chapel had recently disappeared, Hilbre remained in St. Oswald's parish. Later, Hilbre became an extra-parochial liberty of the re-organised Chester city parishes, whose mother church is the 19th century St. Thomas's on Parkgate Road, Chester.[24] Around the turn of the 21st century, Hilbre was moved into the Little Meols parish of St. Andrew, on Meols Drive, between Hoylake and West Kirby.

Hilbre's 'pilgrimage' may have lasted until the Reformation, or been discontinued at some earlier time. The local memories, however, persisted, so that Leyland recorded them, however wrongly, and thus gave the impression in later centuries that a real pilgrimage, medieval style, had existed here. Hume's collection of artefacts from the Meols shore included a number of pilgrim tokens. One, a fragment of a 13th century metal oval from the shrine of Roc St. Amadour was said to have been found at or near Hilbre. Hume deduced from this and other tokens that Hilbre's pilgrimage would have attracted international spiritual travellers.

The French shrine, now Rocamadour, lies on the road to Compostella, one of the most famous European shrines. Having become a victim of France's own Reformation in Napoleonic times,

Rocamadour was revived as a modern pilgrimage site.

As in modern times, however, the possession of a souvenir does not mean that the owner was visiting an equally important and well-known medieval shrine here on Hilbre. He or she may simply have been taking ship to return home from wider travels, and accidentally dropped a treasured possession on the shore.

scale: |_____|

2.5cm

Pilgrim seal of Rocamadour from Hulme, Ancient Meols

The token from Rocamadour, along with many other local finds, was lodged in Liverpool Museum. It appears to have been a casualty of the air raids in the Second World War, which destroyed part of the collection.[25] Only drawings survive.

Recent research in Liverpool Museum and London has suggested that the assemblage of pilgrim tokens recovered from the shore at Meols is typical of a port used by travellers, and not indicative of a nearby shrine.[26]

If Hilbre had hosted a pilgrimage of international importance, it would have been cited in surviving copies of grants and land leases, as were St. Winefride's and other British shrines. There are no known records, in family papers and in the Public Record Office, which suggest that Hilbre received grants specifically for a pilgrim shrine, other than the local Lancelyn family's gifts of a farm and fishing rights to the monks of Hilbre. These do not appear in the Abbey's records to connect with a pilgrimage, but are consistent with the monks' daily lives, concerning food, transport, and the task of fishing for the Abbey.

The third legend: The Lighthouse

The last Earl of Chester, John the Scot, gave at some time in the 1230s, a grant of 10 shillings a year from his treasury, to pay for a light or lights on Hilbre in the chapel of the Blessed Virgin.[27] In the nineteenth century, this light was mistakenly thought to be a beacon for mariners, because a small light can be seen many miles away in clear air. When John the Scot died a few years later, and the line of the Earls ended, the royal family took over the title of Earl of Chester for the heir to the throne. Prince Charles is the current Earl. Payment for the light on Hilbre continued, taken from the coffers of the City of Chester. Instalments were confirmed in 1277, and by 1301, this sum of 10 shillings a year was listed among the Ancient Alms of the Abbey.[28] Eventually, the original purpose of commemoration may have already become out of date, but the grant continued in perpetuity, and was used as part of the Abbey's general charitable income.

After the Abbey became a Cathedral, there was an inquiry in 1545, and the Abbey's Ancient Alms were once again restored, with back-dated payments, to the Cathedral.[29] There was no suggestion that Hilbre's sum of ten shillings a year should continue to support a navigation light or beacon.

The chapel itself apparently disappeared after 1538, when the island was let to a secular landlord.[30] If it had been a beacon, its use would have become even more vital at this time, as from 1540, the shipping records of small coastal sailing vessels, based or harboured at Hilbre, increased greatly in number.[31] Henry VIII began his campaign to subdue Ireland, and used vessels and small ports all along the Wirral coast to transport troops, horses and provisions. The non-existence of a lighthouse on Hilbre at this time suggests that the original lights were not mariners' guides, even though such structures existed in places such as Dover harbour and the Isle of Wight.

St. Catherine's Medieval Lighthouse, Isle of Wight

The light in the Hilbre chapel was more likely to have been a votive lamp, given by John in memory of a relative. It is not unreasonable to suggest that the recipient was his uncle, the previous Earl, Ranulph

III, who had had so much to do with the transfer of Hilbre's chapel to the care of Chester Abbey. Votive lamps, and the payment to a priest to care for them and to say prayers for the deceased, were common in medieval times.[32] Bebington Parish church of St. Andrew still displays four lamp brackets which were said to have held such lights. They could have been fired by olive oil, fish oil or animal fats, such as tallow.

Lamp bracket, Bebington parish church, Wirral

The story of the ten shillings does not end there. The Cathedral's Ancient Alms were used until Victorian times as part of the pool of charitable donations handed out to needy citizens. In 1864, all these payments were gathered together under Chester's Council, and a capital sum invested, whose interest would pay the recipients of the charities from that time onwards.[33] Hilbre's ten shillings disappeared into a joint sum, but was never truly discontinued in spirit. Today, the payments are administered by a firm of Chester solicitors, and the Chester Municipal Charities continue to receive requests for help from local people. Hilbre may not have had a lighthouse, but John the Scot's legacy is still with us.

Rumours of a lost Roman lighthouse or signalling station on Hilbre seem to have arisen in the 19th century, when a local scholar described his studies of Roman remains in the Mediterranean. He remarked that Hilbre would have been a good place for such a building, as it guarded the Dee estuary. No Roman buildings or archaeology have been detected on Hilbre, except for about 25 fragments of grey domestic pottery, dating from about the 2nd century AD.

These were found by R. Newstead during his archaeological survey of 1925, sponsored by the Royden family of Frankby.[33b] Whether these are sufficient evidence for a military presence on Hilbre is debatable.

Roman pottery found by R. Newstead in 1926

(Photograph by Eric Hosking, reproduced by kind permission of the Eric Hosking Trust)

The fourth legend: the chapel bell from Hilbre

St. Oswald's parish church in Bidston used to have a 16th century bell among its peal, which was recast in 1868.[34] The original bell bore an inscription 'Sancti Oswaldi. C.W: J.W: W.W.' At some time, a tale grew up that this bell came not from St. Oswald's in Chester, where similar bells were sold off in 1551, but from the chapel on Hilbre. Certainly, Hilbre was in St. Oswald's parish, and there may have been a bell hung inside the building or in a bell-cote on the roof.

There is no record of what happened to the chapel on Hilbre after 1538, when Thomas Birkhead's lease was intended to last for 60 years. The lease was shortly transferred to the Stanleys of Hooton, who ran a shipping centre for travellers, cargo and troop movements from Hilbre.[35] The chapel may have survived, deconsecrated, as a barn or warehouse. One of the last monks was allowed to live on Hilbre in his retirement, dying in 1550.[36] If the monks' house had been taken over as his home or as a shipping office, then it is possible that the old barns and the chapel became storage places.

Another of St. Oswald's bells from the sale in 1551 was almost certainly the bell which went to

Conwy parish church, its price of £33 being recorded in the Cathedral accounts. It still hangs in the church belfry at Conwy, with a dedication to St. Werburgh, also naming John Birkenshawe.[37] He was the last but one Abbot at Chester, when the political troubles of the Reformation were beginning, and the Abbey was looking to protect its lands and possessions by leasing them out.

In a recent conversation, the Rev. Jones of Conwy suggested that bells from Chester would have been carried by water to their new homes. Therefore the Dee, and Hilbre as a stopping place could have been the route for transporting both Bidston's and Conwy's new acquisitions. The Bidston bell may have come via Hilbre, but possibly not from the chapel. If it had indeed hung on Hilbre, it could have been returned to Chester when the island's chapel was abandoned. This would have happened in 1538, if at all, and the bell sold 13 years later from Chester.

Medieval bell from Worcester Cathedral

The fifth legend: The Constable Sands

A sixteenth century monk at Chester Abbey, Henry Bradshawe, wrote a story which was probably already a folk tale of the time.[38] It told how Earl Richard (1101 - 1120) on a journey to the shrine of St. Winefride was attacked by a band of Welsh marauders, and sent a messenger to fetch his Constable with a boat to rescue him. The Constable, William Fitz Nigel of Halton Castle, reached Hilbre, as the nearest port on the Cheshire shore, but found no ship there. He appealed to a monk for help, and was told to pray to St. Werburgh, whereupon the tide drew back from the sands of Dee and allowed him to cross and rescue his lord. The Priory of Norton near Runcorn, in Fitz Nigel's demesne, was said to have been founded in gratitude.

The story may contain some truths. The sands were often fordable at various points along the Dee, especially between Shotwick and Flint. A guide was usually needed, as in crossing Morecambe Bay nowadays. The route was almost obliterated by the construction of the New Cut in the course of the River Dee in 1732, but intrepid walkers have since crossed at times of unusually low spring tides. In another legend, set in Hugh Blundeville's time, the Earl's ship, threatened by a storm, was saved at midnight by the regular night prayers of the Chester monks. Control of the tides and storms was believed to lie in the power of these holy men.[39]

The presence of monks on Hilbre in 1115 or thereabouts was unlikely, as the island was at this time in the possession of St. Evroult's Abbey. The time of the incident was therefore probably in the following century, if it took place at all. It is interesting that the monk advised Fitz Nigel to pray to St. Werburgh, and not to St. Mary, the island chapel's saint, nor to St. Hildeburgh. If Norton Priory owed its foundation to this rescue, such gestures of thankfulness were not unusual in the Middle Ages.

The sixth legend: The Lady's Cave

A cave in the western cliffs on the main island has been called the Lady's Cave for some time. A niece of the housekeeper to the Hilbre Island Club, lessees of the former Trinity House building until the 1930s, said that a ship's figurehead was washed up here, and so gave the cave its name. A wooden figurehead, probably this one, stood in the garden of Trinity Cottage until the 1940s. A similar carving is now displayed in the Maritime Museum, Liverpool.

Colonel Egerton Leigh collected folk tales of Cheshire, one about the daughter of the castellan of Shotwick.[40] She was sailing to Wales for an arranged marriage, against her will, and threw herself overboard. There are other versions but all end with her being washed up in the cave, and telling her story to a monk, in whose arms she then died. No one has solved the mystery of this sad tale. If there is any truth, it can be dated very approximately by the presence of a monk, from about 1140 onwards, and by the dates during which Shotwick Castle was maintained as a royal fortress, protecting the Welsh crossing, between the 12th and 14th centuries.[41]

The story of the chapel and its grave markers

Beginning with Orderic's account of the 11th century gift of Hilbre and other properties, by Robert of Rhuddlan to St. Evroult's Abbey in Normandy, there were later references to the chapel of St. Mary, as in the grants of Ancient Alms to the Abbey of St. Werburgh.[42] It therefore really existed, although we cannot say how it looked, nor when it was built.

Orderic was the third son of a Norman family, and he was at school in Shrewsbury as a young child from about 1080. Returning to Normandy in about 1085 when he was ten (and speaking only English) he became a resident at St. Evroult's Abbey.

Eventually he became a monk, and was a prolific writer and chronicler, noting grants and gifts to his abbey, among which were West Kirby with Hilbre and other properties, including St. Peter's church in Chester, and the parishes of Byfield and Marston St. Lawrence in Northamptonshire. He is a major source of information about the Norman noblemen of Cheshire.[43]

St. Evroult's Abbey, having owned the title to West Kirby and Hilbre for about 60 years, transferred it in about 1140 along with other properties to St. Werburgh's in Chester.[44] Whether there were monks on Hilbre at this point is not known, although the chapel on Hildeburgheye is mentioned. The Norman abbey retained its right to payment for the estates, known as 'residuary rent', which was claimed

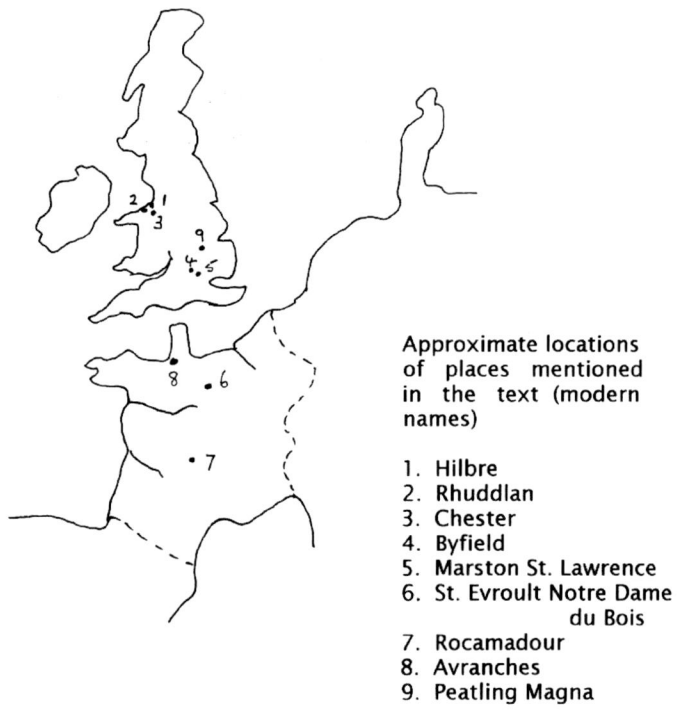

Approximate locations of places mentioned in the text (modern names)

1. Hilbre
2. Rhuddlan
3. Chester
4. Byfield
5. Marston St. Lawrence
6. St. Evroult Notre Dame du Bois
7. Rocamadour
8. Avranches
9. Peatling Magna

probably until Henry V's Act of Alienation of Priories in 1414 deprived foreign religious houses of their often long-standing rights in such as rents and tithes in England. From 1140, St. Werburgh's monks were required to travel to Peatling Magna in Leicestershire, another manor of St. Evroult's, to pay the residual rent for West Kirby and Hilbre, of 30 shillings a year.[45] St. Evroult's asserted its right to interfere at intervals when West Kirby, although now separated from Hilbre, continued to be the focus for legal battles between Chester Abbey and St.

Mary's Abbey in Basingwerk.[46] St. Evroult's Abbey was dissolved in the 18th century French Revolution and its ruins lie in the modern village of St. Evroult Notre Dame du Bois, near Gaceċ in the department of Orne.[47]

The ruins of St. Evroult's Abbey, Normandy
(Photograph by Allen and Barbara Burton)

In 1852, Mr. Hughes, one of the Victorian telegraph keepers, dug up a piece of sandstone on the top of Hilbre, while collecting materials to repair the trackway. His little daughter was credited with finding it, but probably she merely drew attention to the deeply carved surface of the stone. It was a fragment of a Saxon wheel head cross, taken into the care of Canon Abraham Hulme, in Liverpool, and handed to Mr. W.E. Shrubsole of Chester

Archaeological Society.[48] Placed in the Grosvenor Museum in Chester, it is now displayed there.

This style of Saxon cross, dating from about 1000 AD, with Scandinavian influences, has been found in many churches in Wirral, Chester and North Wales. Most of these surviving crosses are in pieces, having been broken up by Norman builders, less than a century after they were placed over the graves of local people. Used as building material, the pieces were rediscovered by Victorian church restorers. The Hilbre fragment is about two thirds of the circular head. The base has never been found, so it is just possible that this portion was carried to the island early in the Middle Ages from West Kirby parish church, to be re-used as building stone on Hilbre. There are several cross fragments on view at St. Bridget's, discovered in the walls during rebuilding of the medieval church in 1869. Accounts of the Wirral crosses were written by Bu'lock and Collingwood.[49]

|---------| c. 10 cm

Hilbre's cross head in the Grosvenor Museum, Chester

The second discovery, about 10 years later, was also made by Mr. Hughes, helped by Henry Ecroyd Smith, and described in 1865. Like the first cross it was a grave marker, but neither find was recorded in detail. The four bodies found under the second stone, a grey sandstone slab, and its position on the island have both been lost, in spite of rather vague descriptions in several of Ecroyd Smith's publications. Fortunately, about two thirds of the stone survived in use as a gate post on Hilbre, and was then built into the wall of a shed. It was retrieved by William Fergusson Irvine in 1914 at the request of the Dock Board, and placed in the Charles Dawson Brown museum at St. Bridget's church, as recorded in the Mersey Docks and Harbour Board Minutes.[50] The slab was reconstructed in an illustration in Brownbill's book.

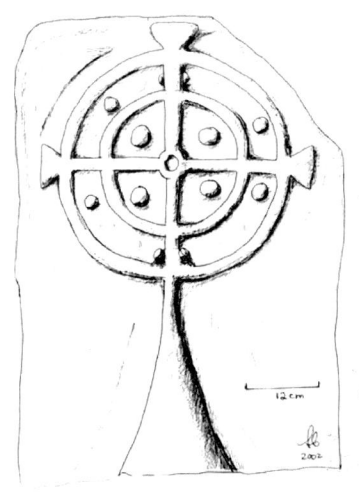

|----------| c. 10 cm

Author's reconstruction of grave slab from Hilbre c.1100

It is likely that the grave stone covered an original burial on Hilbre, and was not recycled stone from the mainland, as it would have been more difficult to transport intact to Hilbre, rather than broken up into re-usable pieces. The original interred body was not identified, and described merely as an adult male, although the stone could be dated to about 1100 AD by its style.[51] The other bodies had been added hurriedly at the side of the slab, according to Ecroyd Smith.[52] They may have been victims of drowning, interred informally in a holy place near to the monks' chapel, after Hilbre lost its right to receive burials, a result of Rector William's agreement of the 1230s.

Medieval beads of glass and clay were occasionally found in the turf or gardens on Hilbre, and one of these is now in Liverpool Museum.[53] It is a blue glass bead with coloured trails of green and yellow and is typical of Saxon grave goods. Others could possibly have been rosary beads, lost on Hilbre when its chapel was staffed by monks, and visited by local residents.

Saxon bead from Hilbre   scale: 1 cm

A final word

Considering Hilbre's past, is it so bad to have a few unfounded legends? St. George inspires many people who know that the real man was probably a bishop in the Middle East, whose image became linked with that of a mythical figure representing the fight between Good and Evil. So long as we remember what is fact and what is fancy, we can enjoy the stories!

Much of Hilbre's early history is probably lost forever, but there are hints about what was happening in Wirral and Cheshire as a whole in the early Middle Ages.

Some Saxon churches were probably founded in Wirral by the 10th century, including St. Bridget's in West Kirby, Eastham, Overchurch, Woodchurch, Neston and others. The survival of carved stones like the Hilbre wheel head cross shows that there was a thriving Christian community in Wirral and the rest of Cheshire before the Norman Conquest, and that the style of their carved monuments was a combination of Saxon and Scandinavian forms.

West Kirby's relative wealth after the Conquest suggests that it was an important parish centre. Despite its transfer to a French abbey in 1080, possibly with the intention of setting up an outpost here in Northern England, it never developed further. The property was a long way from France, and West Kirby lands and church rights were returned to English hands when Chester Abbey received Hilbre (and more briefly, West Kirby) into its list of estates.

What were the monks of Hilbre doing? We can only guess that their duties included watching that this small but useful island was not taken over by other claimants, such as Basingwerk Abbey. The monks certainly collected tithes from West Kirby and nearby villages, and carried them, probably by boat, to the abbey in Chester. It is more than likely they caught fish for the Abbey tables, as two boats were still in use at the Reformation, which were worked by the resident monks' servants.

Benedictines were and are a practical religious order. While prayers in the island chapel were important, the job of running a working outpost of the abbey on Hilbre would have been an important function

Shaft of a grave marker from St. Bridget's parish church, West Kirby, of the same period as the Hilbre cross head, showing the style of carving with Saxon and Scandinavian influences, c. 1000

(drawing from H. E. Smith, A conventual cemetery)

Once Hilbre was settled as an outpost of the abbey in Chester, staffed by 2 of its own monks, the threat of Basingwerk Abbey's claim became less. The other challenge, of a land-hungry rector, whose family continued to follow up their claim almost until

1400, was largely dealt with in the 1230s, a very busy time.

The last of the rector's family in West Kirby was relieved of his duties on Hilbre, in return for a promise to his successors of an annual service, dimly remembered in later stories. Rectors after the 1230s were appointed by Chester Abbey, and not by their own relatives, and a lamp was placed in the island chapel, possibly as a votive or prayer lamp, and almost certainly with no relation to shipping.

Gifts of a farm and fishing rights by the Lancelyn Green family ensured supplies of food, horses for transport, and increased fisheries to help the management of Hilbre as a small monastic estate.

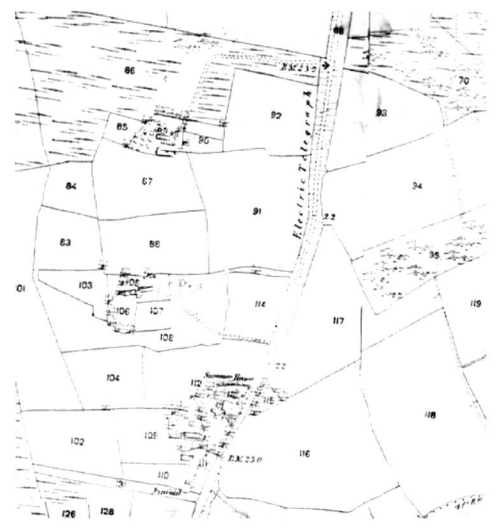

Ordnance Survey Map of Little Meols surveyed in 1871, showing some of the old farms near to the present Royal Liverpool Golf Course and Meols Drive (here the path of the domestic electric telegraph cable)

After Henry VIII's reformation of the church, Hilbre lost its religious ties, and became an important maritime centre, largely because of its closeness to the natural harbour of Hoyle Lake. As a source of rental income to Chester Cathedral, it evidently proved useful for the next 300 years, until changing times and the rise of Liverpool's Atlantic trade attracted the Mersey city merchants to buy Hilbre's freehold title in 1856.

With the loss of Hoyle Lake, due to movements of the sand banks, and the effects of dredging in the Mersey approaches, Hilbre ceased to be a landing place No doubt there was smuggling, as there still is in many parts of Britain. Local inhabitants may have resented Hilbre's tenants, when trying to claim fishing rights, access to the island, and the use of stone or gravel from the shore. There are records of all these quarrels up to the 19th century. But these stories are the stuff of daily life, not of dramatic legend!

Map of the main island of Hilbre today

REFERENCES

[1] J. D. Craggs, *Hilbre, the Cheshire Island*, (Liverpool University Press,1982), p. 47.

[2] John Tait, *The Chartulary or Register of the Abbey of St. Werburgh*, (Chetham Society, New Series, 1922), vols. 79 and 82.

[3] Samuel Fearon, and John Eyes, *Description of the Sea Coast of England and North Wales*, Liverpool, 1737, (2nd Edition 1755), Liverpool Record Office, ref. Hf 386.35 FEA.

[4] R. Newstead, 'The Excavations at Hilbre 1926', *Transactions of the Historic Society of Lancashire and Cheshire*, New Series, vol.78, (1926), pp. 136 - 143.

[5] J. McNeil Dodgson, *The Place Names of Cheshire*, (English Place Name Society, Cambridge University Press 1972), vol. 47, p. 302.

[6] Canon A. Hume, *Finds at Ancient Meols*, (John Russell Smith, London 1863)

[7] Henry Ecroyd Smith, Notice of an early conventual cemetry in Wirral, *Transactions of the Historic Society of Lancashire and Cheshire*, vol. 17, p. 271 - 276 (1865); Reliques of the Anglo Saxon Churches of St. Bridget and St.Hildeburga, West Kirby, *Transactions of the Historic Society of Lancashire and Cheshire*, vol. 23. (1870).

[8] Tait, *Chartulary*, vol. 82, pp. 289, 298-9.

[9] Marjorie Chibnall, (ed.), *The ecclesiastical history of Orderic Vitalis*, in 6 vols, (Clarendon Press, Oxford 1980), Vol.III, p.238, f 4, Vol.VI, p. 304.

[10] George Ormerod, *The History of the County Palatine of Chester*, (2nd edition 1882, ed. Thomas Helsby), vol. 1, p. 8.
[11] John Leland, *Itinerary of England 1535 - 43*, (ed.) T. Smith, in 5 vols., (London 1907 - 1910). Vol. III, pp. 91, 92.
[12] R. V. H. Burne, *The Monks of Chester*, (SPCK, London 1962), p. 59.
[13] W. H. Bliss, (ed.), *Calendar of Papal Registers and Papal Letters*, vol. I, 1198 - 1304, vol. II, 1305 - 1342, vol. III 1342 - 1362, (HMSO 1895)
[14] Tait, *Chartulary*, vols 79 and 82.
[15] Tait (1922), Chartulary, Chetham Soc Papers vols 79 and 82.
[16] Brownbill, *West Kirby*, p. 89.
[17] Brownbill, *West Kirby*, p. 92.
[18] Brownbill, *West Kirby*, pp. 196 - 199.
[19] John Day, *All Saints' Church, Peatling Magna*, Church Guide, (1999), p.3.
[20] Brownbill, *West Kirby*, pp 102 - 103.
[21] Tait (1922), *Chartulary*, Chetham Soc Papers, vol. 82, p. 296, item 515.
[22] Brownbill, *West Kirby*, p. 199.
[23] Burne, *Monks*, pp. 23-4, 91.
[24] St. Oswald's Parish records, Cheshire CRO. Reference P/29.
[25] Personal communication, Christine Longworth, Liverpool Museum, 2003.
[26] Personal communication, Rob Philpott, Liverpool Museum, 2004.
[27] Tait, *Chartulary*, vol. 79, p. 299; Brownbill, West Kirby, p. 167.

[28] *Cheshire Sheaf* (1909), 3rd Series, vol. 7, p 43, Item 1316.
[29] *Cheshire Sheaf*, (1909), 3rd Series, vol. 7, p 43, Item 1316;
R.V. H. Burne, Chester Cathedral, (SPCK, London 1958), p. 20.
[30] Burne, *Monks*, p. 179.
[31] Brownbill, *West Kirby*, p. 36 - 37.
[32] Charles W. Budden, *Rambles round the old churches of Wirral*, (Edward Howell, Liverpool, 1922), p. 159.
[33] W. Brown, *A History of the Municipal Charities of Chester from 1837 - 1875*, (Chester, 1875), Chester Public Library, ref.
[33b] R. Newstead, *Transactions of the Historic Society of Lancashire and Cheshire*, New Series, vol. 78, pp. 136-143.
[34] Phillip Sulley, *The Hundred of Wirral*, published by the author, (B. Haram & Co., Birkenhead 1889), p. 331;
Budden, *Rambles*, p. 45.
[35] *Cheshire Sheaf*, (1902), New Series, vol. 4, p. 43, Item 624.
[36] *Cheshire Sheaf*, (1921), New Series, vol. 18, p. 75, Item 4404.
[37] Burne, *Cathedral*, p. 23.
[38] Brownbill, *West Kirby*, pp. 29-30.
[39] Ormerod, *History*, p 34.
[40] Egerton Leigh, *Ballads of Cheshire*, p. 119;
Personal communications, Mrs. Meredith and Mrs. Parkinson, Wirral 2002-4.
[41] Whitfield, Lavinia, *The Church at the Ford*, 2nd Edition, (Local publication, 1976); Shotwick Church Guide.

[42] Burne, *Cathedral*, p. 20; *Cheshire Sheaf*, (1909), 3rd Series, vii, p 43, Item 1316.
[43] Chibnall, *Orderic*, Vol. II, p. 260, Vol. VI, p. 304.
[44] Brownbill, *West Kirby*, pp. 88 - 89.
[45] Tait, *Chartulary*, vol. 82, pp. 289 - 291; Brownbill, *West Kirby*, pp. 88-89.
[46] Brownbill, *West Kirby*, pp. 94 - 96.
[47] Personal communication, The Custodian, Ermitage Notre Dame, St. Evroult Notre Dame du Bois, Normandy, 1997.
[48] Hume, *Ancient Meols*, p. 267.
[49] J. D. Bu'lock, *Pre-Conquest Cheshire, 383 - 1066*, (Cheshire Community Council, Chester, 1972), p. 82, plate 20.
[50] Mersey Docks and Harbour Board Minutes for 1914, Liverpool Maritime Museum, ref. Marine Agenda, in Bound Volume no. 1 Hilbre.
[51] W. G. Collingwood, in Brownbill, *West Kirby*, p. 22.
[52] Henry Ecroyd Smith, 'Notice of an early conventual cemetery in Wirral', *Transactions of the Historic Society of Lancashire and Cheshire*, vol. 17, (1865), pp. 271 - 276.
[53] Hume, *Ancient Meols*, pp. 162 - 163.

Hilbre's Saxon cross